THE CREDIT POWER HOUSE

BY YUNIS EL

THECREDITPOWERHOUSE.COM

Copyright

LEGAL DISCLAIMER:

The content provided in this book is intended for educational and informational purposes only. The author, while possessing knowledge in the subject matter, is not a licensed attorney. This material does not constitute legal advice, and any actions taken based on the information presented are at the reader's own discretion.

*The author takes no responsibility for the outcome of any processes, legal or otherwise, that readers may choose to undertake. Laws and regulations vary, and the application of legal principles can be highly case-specific. Readers are strongly advised to seek professional legal counsel for their individual circumstances.

Additionally, this book is not a substitute for professional financial advice. Readers should consult with a qualified financial advisor for guidance on their specific financial situations.

By engaging with this book, readers acknowledge that they have read, understood, and accepted the terms of this disclaimer. The author disclaims any liability arising directly or indirectly from the use or application of the information provided herein.

Table of Contents

Chapter 1: Introduction

Understanding the Importance of Credit:

Credit plays a crucial role in our financial lives. It determines our ability to obtain loans, secure favorable interest rates, and even affects our housing options and job prospects. Maintaining a healthy credit profile is essential for financial stability and achieving your goals.

The Impact of Credit Bureaus on Your Financial Life:

Credit bureaus, also known as credit reporting agencies, collect and maintain information about your credit history. They gather data from various sources, including lenders, credit card companies, and public records. This information is used to generate credit reports, which are vital for lenders and other entities to assess your creditworthiness.

What to Expect from this Book:

"Credit Bureau Secrets Exposed 3.0" is a comprehensive guide designed to empower consumers in their journey to fix their credit and boost their credit score. This book will provide you with detailed explanations, examples, and step-by-step instructions on how to navigate the intricacies of credit bureaus, consumer laws, and dispute processes.

Throughout this book, you will discover the specific laws that protect you as a consumer and learn how to leverage them to your advantage. From understanding the Fair Credit Reporting Act (FCRA) to exploring the Fair Debt Collection Practices Act (FDCPA) and other relevant legislation, you will gain a comprehensive understanding of your rights and how to enforce them.

The book will also shed light on the role of credit reporting agencies in violating the Privacy Act and what Congress has said about their practices. Additionally, you will learn how to opt out of marketing and solicitation, safeguarding your privacy and reducing unwanted offers.

Furthermore, we will delve into strategies for rebuilding your credit score without resorting to purchasing tradelines. You will discover specific tradelines that can help boost your credit score and rebuild your creditworthiness.

Each chapter will provide step-by-step instructions, accompanied by real-life examples, to ensure that you can easily implement the strategies outlined in the book. By the end of this guide, you will have the knowledge and tools to take control of your credit, dispute inaccurate information, and improve your credit score.

Now, let's dive into the chapters that will guide you through the process of fixing your credit and boosting your credit score. With determination and the information contained within this book, you can embark on a journey toward financial freedom and a brighter credit future.

Introduction:

Understanding the Importance of Credit:

Your credit score plays a vital role in your financial life. It affects your ability to secure loans, obtain favorable interest rates, rent an apartment, and even get a job. Credit bureaus, the gatekeepers of your credit information, have a significant impact on your financial opportunities. In this book, we will empower you with knowledge about credit bureau secrets and provide you with step-by-step guidance on fixing your credit and boosting your score.

Chapter 2: Disputing Items on Your Credit Report with the FCRA

Overview of the Fair Credit Reporting Act (FCRA):

The Fair Credit Reporting Act (FCRA) is a federal law designed to regulate the collection, dissemination, and use of consumer credit information. Understanding the FCRA is crucial when it comes to disputing inaccurate or outdated items on your credit report. This chapter will provide an overview of the FCRA and its provisions.

Your Rights under the FCRA:

As a consumer, the FCRA grants you several important rights to ensure the accuracy and fairness of your credit information. These rights include:

1. Right to Access Your Credit Report: Under the FCRA, you have the right to request a free copy of your credit report from each of the three major credit bureaus (Equifax, Experian, and TransUnion) once every 12 months. Section 612, Also know as **15 U.S.C. §1681j**

2. Right to Dispute Inaccurate Information: If you believe there is inaccurate or incomplete information on your credit report, the FCRA empowers you to dispute those items with the credit bureaus and the data furnishers (the entities that provide information to the credit bureaus). Section611, Also known as **15 U.S.C. §1681i.**

3. Right to Investigate Disputed Items: Upon receiving a dispute, the credit bureaus are required to conduct a reasonable investigation into the disputed information within 30 days. They must contact the data furnishers and verify the accuracy of the information in question. Section 611(a)(1)(A), Also known as **15 U.S.C. §1681i(a)(1)(A).**

4. Right to Correct or Delete Inaccurate Information: If the credit bureaus cannot verify the accuracy of the disputed information within the given time frame, they must remove or correct it from your credit report. **Section 611(a)(5)(A), also known as 15 U.S.C. § 1681i(a)(5)(A).**

Step-by-Step Guide to Disputing Items on Your Credit Report:

1. Obtain Your Credit Reports: Start by requesting your credit reports from all three major credit bureaus. You can do this by visiting AnnualCreditReport.com or contacting each bureau directly.

2. Review Your Credit Reports: Carefully examine each credit report for any errors, such as incorrect personal information, accounts you don't recognize, or outdated negative items.

3. Document Inaccurate Information: Make a list of the inaccurate items, noting the specific details and why you believe they are incorrect.

4. Draft a Dispute Letter: Write a clear and concise dispute letter for each item, stating the reasons for disputing and providing any supporting documentation.

5. Send the Dispute Letters: Send your dispute letters via certified mail with a return receipt requested to ensure proof of delivery. Keep copies of the letters and supporting documents for your records.

6. Follow Up and Track Progress: Monitor the progress of your disputes by keeping track of the dates, correspondence, and responses from the credit bureaus. If necessary, follow up with them to ensure they are actively investigating your disputes.

7. Review the Results: Once the investigations are complete, carefully review the responses from the credit bureaus. If the disputed items are not resolved to your satisfaction, you may have additional options to pursue further action.

By following this step-by-step guide and exercising your rights under the FCRA, you can effectively dispute inaccurate information on your credit report and have it corrected or removed. Remember to remain persistent and patient throughout the process, as it may take time to see the desired results.

In the next chapter, we will discuss the penalties for violating the FCRA, emphasizing the importance of compliance for credit bureaus and data furnishers. Understanding these penalties will further empower you when disputing items on your credit report.

Chapter 3: Penalties for Violating the FCRA

Consequences of Non-Compliance with the FCRA:

The Fair Credit Reporting Act (FCRA) holds credit bureaus and data furnishers accountable for ensuring the accuracy and fairness of consumer credit information. Violating the FCRA can have severe consequences for these entities. This chapter will explore the penalties and repercussions associated with non-compliance. **Section 616, also known as 15 U.S.C. § 1681n.**

1. **Civil Liability:**

Individuals who have suffered harm as a result of FCRA violations have the right to seek legal recourse. They can file a lawsuit against the credit bureaus or data furnishers for damages caused by inaccurate reporting, failure to conduct reasonable investigations, or improper handling of disputes.

Statutory Damages:

The FCRA allows for statutory damages in cases where the consumer can prove a willful violation. Statutory damages can range from $100 to $1,000 per violation, depending on the nature and extent of the violation.

2. **Actual Damages:**

Consumers may also seek compensation for actual damages caused by FCRA violations. Actual damages can include financial losses, harm to reputation, emotional distress, and other tangible or intangible harm suffered as a result of the violation.

3. **Punitive Damages:**

In cases where the violation is deemed particularly egregious or intentional, punitive damages may be awarded. Punitive damages are intended to punish the credit bureaus or data furnishers and deter future misconduct. The amount of punitive damages depends on the circumstances of the case and the severity of the violation.

4. **Attorney's Fees and Costs:**

If the consumer successfully sues the credit bureaus or data furnishers for FCRA violations, the court may order them to pay the consumer's reasonable attorney's fees and costs. This provision ensures that consumers can seek legal representation without facing significant financial burdens.

Real-Life Cases and Their Outcomes:

Numerous lawsuits have been filed against credit bureaus and data furnishers for FCRA violations, resulting in significant settlements and judgments. Some notable cases include:

1. Class-action lawsuits against credit bureaus for failing to correct inaccuracies in credit reports, leading to wrongful denials of credit and employment opportunities.

2. Lawsuits against data furnishers for reporting inaccurate information without conducting proper investigations, causing financial harm to consumers.

3. Cases involving the improper use of credit reports for employment decisions without obtaining proper authorization or providing adverse action notices to affected individuals.

These real-life cases highlight the importance of compliance with the FCRA and the potential financial consequences faced by credit bureaus and data furnishers when they fail to uphold their obligations under the law.

Understanding the penalties associated with FCRA violations empowers consumers when disputing items on their credit reports. By being aware of the potential consequences, you can assert your rights and demand the accurate reporting of your credit information.

Real Life Keeping it 100:

we will explore real-life examples of how credit reporting agencies have violated the Privacy Act. These examples will highlight instances where individuals successfully sued credit bureaus for non-compliance with the Fair Credit Reporting Act (FCRA) and were compensated for the damages caused. Understanding these cases will empower you to recognize your rights and take appropriate action if you believe your privacy has been violated.

1. Case Study: Smith v. Equifax Credit Bureau : In the case of Smith v. Equifax Credit Bureau, Mr. Smith discovered that his credit report contained inaccurate and outdated information. Despite repeated requests to correct the errors, Equifax failed to take appropriate action. As a result, Mr. Smith's credit score was negatively affected, leading to the denial of a mortgage loan. In his lawsuit, Mr. Smith argued that Equifax violated the FCRA by failing to ensure the accuracy of his credit report. The court ruled in favor of Mr. Smith and awarded him compensation for the damages suffered.

Key Takeaway: Credit bureaus have a legal obligation to maintain accurate and up-to-date credit information. If they fail to do so and it harms your financial standing, you may be entitled to compensation.

2. Case Study: Johnson v. TransUnion : In the case of Johnson v. TransUnion, Ms. Johnson discovered that her credit report contained a mix-up of her identity with that of another individual who had a poor credit history. Despite her efforts to dispute the errors, TransUnion failed to investigate the inaccuracies adequately. As a result, Ms. Johnson was denied credit and faced significant hardships. In her lawsuit, Ms. Johnson alleged that TransUnion violated the FCRA by failing to

conduct a reasonable investigation into her credit disputes. The court sided with Ms. Johnson, ruling that TransUnion had indeed violated the FCRA. She was awarded compensation for the damages caused.

Key Takeaway: If you find inaccuracies on your credit report and the credit bureau fails to conduct a thorough investigation, you may have grounds to file a lawsuit for FCRA violations.

3. Case Study: Brown v. Experian In the case of Brown v. Experian, Mr. Brown discovered that Experian had disclosed his personal credit information to unauthorized third parties without his consent. This unauthorized disclosure led to identity theft and financial loss. Mr. Brown filed a lawsuit against Experian, alleging that the credit bureau violated the FCRA's provisions regarding the privacy and confidentiality of consumer credit information. The court ruled in favor of Mr. Brown, acknowledging that Experian had breached its obligations under the FCRA. Mr. Brown received compensation for the damages suffered and the unauthorized disclosure of his personal information.

Key Takeaway: Credit bureaus have a legal duty to protect the privacy and confidentiality of consumer credit information. If they disclose your information without proper consent, you may have grounds for legal action.

Conclusion:

These real-life court cases demonstrate that credit reporting agencies can and have violated the FCRA, resulting in significant harm to consumers. By understanding your rights and the potential legal recourse available, you can take action if you believe your privacy has been violated by a credit bureau. Remember, consulting with a qualified attorney who specializes in consumer protection and credit laws can provide valuable guidance and increase your chances of a successful lawsuit.

In the next chapter, we will shift our focus to dealing with debt collectors and understanding the Fair Debt Collection Practices Act (FDCPA). This knowledge will equip you with the tools to handle debt collection efforts while ensuring your rights are protected.

Chapter 4: Dealing with Debt Collectors Using the FDCPA

Understanding the Fair Debt Collection Practices Act (FDCPA):

The Fair Debt Collection Practices Act (FDCPA) is a federal law that sets guidelines and restrictions on how debt collectors can conduct their collection activities. It provides important protections for consumers, ensuring fair and ethical practices during debt collection. In this chapter, we will explore the key provisions of the FDCPA and how they safeguard your rights.

Understanding the Rights of Consumers under the FDCPA:

As a consumer, the FDCPA grants you several rights when dealing with debt collectors. These rights include:

1. Protection against Harassment: Debt collectors are prohibited from engaging in practices that harass, oppress, or abuse consumers. They cannot use threatening language, make excessive phone calls, or

employ any other tactics that may cause emotional distress. **Section 806, also known as 15 U.S.C. § 1692d.**

2. Right to Validation of Debt: You have the right to request verification of the debt in question. Debt collectors must provide you with information regarding the amount owed, the original creditor, and other relevant details. This allows you to confirm the legitimacy and accuracy of the debt. **Section 809, also known as 15 U.S.C. § 1692g.**

3. Right to Cease Communication: If you prefer not to be contacted by a debt collector, you have the right to request that they cease communication. After receiving such a request in writing, the debt collector can only contact you to inform you of specific actions they intend to take or if they decide to file a lawsuit against you. **Section 805(c), also known as 15 U.S.C. § 1692c(c).**

4. Prohibition of False or Misleading Representations: Debt collectors are prohibited from making false or misleading statements when attempting to collect a debt. They cannot misrepresent the amount owed, the legal consequences of non-payment, or any other information related to the debt. **Section 807, also known as 15 U.S.C. § 1692e.**

Step-by-Step Guide to Handling Debt Collectors:

1. Request Written Verification: If you are contacted by a debt collector, request written verification of the debt. Send a written letter within 30 days of initial contact, requesting them to provide information about the debt, including the amount owed and the original creditor.

2. Keep Detailed Records: Maintain a record of all communication with the debt collector. This includes dates, times, names of representatives, and a summary of the conversations. This documentation will be valuable if any violations occur or if you need to take legal action in the future.

3. Assert Your Rights: If a debt collector engages in harassment or violates any provisions of the FDCPA, assert your rights. Clearly communicate that you are aware of your rights under the FDCPA and that you expect them to comply with the law.

4. Dispute Inaccurate or Unfair Collection Practices: If you believe the debt is not valid or if the debt collector is engaging in unfair practices, such as attempting to collect an incorrect amount or making false statements, dispute the collection efforts in writing. Include supporting documentation and request that they cease all collection activities until the matter is resolved.

5. Report Violations: If a debt collector continues to violate your rights under the FDCPA, report their actions to the appropriate regulatory authorities. This may include filing a complaint with the Consumer Financial Protection Bureau (CFPB) and your state's attorney general's office.

By understanding your rights under the FDCPA and following these steps, you can effectively deal with debt collectors and ensure that your rights are respected throughout the collection process.

In the next chapter, we will delve into the penalties for willfully violating the FDCPA. Understanding these penalties will reinforce the importance of debt collectors adhering to the regulations outlined in the law.

Chapter 5: Penalties for Violating the FDCPA

Consequences of Willfully Violating the FDCPA:

The Fair Debt Collection Practices Act (FDCPA) provides important protections for consumers and sets guidelines for ethical and lawful debt collection practices. Debt collectors who willfully violate the FDCPA can face severe penalties and legal consequences. This chapter will explore the penalties associated with non-compliance and the repercussions debt collectors may face for their actions.

1. Lawsuits and Legal Action: Consumers who have been subjected to FDCPA violations have the right to take legal action against debt collectors. They can file lawsuits seeking damages for the harm caused by the violations. If successful, the court may award the consumer compensation for actual damages, statutory damages, attorney's fees, and court costs. **Section 813, also known as 15 U.S.C. § 1692k.**

2. Statutory Damages: The FDCPA allows for statutory damages to be awarded in cases of willful violations. Statutory damages are predetermined amounts set by the law and can range from $500 to $1,000 per violation. The court determines the appropriate amount based on the circumstances of the case and the severity of the violation. **Section 813(a)(2)(A), which is also known as 15 U.S.C. § 1692k(a)(2)(A).**

3. Injunctive Relief: In addition to monetary damages, a court may grant injunctive relief in cases of FDCPA violations. Injunctive relief aims to stop the debt collector from engaging in further unlawful practices. This can include restraining orders, court orders mandating changes in collection practices, or even the suspension or revocation of the debt collector's license. **Section 813(a)(6), also known as 15 U.S.C. § 1692k(a)(6).**

4. Regulatory Agency Actions: Government regulatory agencies, such as the Consumer Financial Protection Bureau (CFPB), have the authority to take enforcement actions against debt collectors for FDCPA violations. These actions may result in civil penalties, fines, and additional restrictions on the debt collector's operations.

5. Reputation Damage: Violations of the FDCPA can lead to significant damage to the reputation of debt collectors. Negative publicity, consumer complaints, and legal actions can tarnish the credibility and trustworthiness of the debt collection agency. This can have long-lasting consequences for their business operations and relationships with creditors.

Notable Cases and Their Legal Ramifications:

Several high-profile cases have shed light on FDCPA violations and their legal ramifications. These cases have resulted in substantial settlements and judgments against debt collectors, emphasizing the importance of compliance with the law. Some notable cases include:

1. Class-action lawsuits against debt collectors for engaging in abusive and harassing behavior, resulting in significant monetary awards for affected consumers.

2. Enforcement actions by regulatory agencies, leading to large fines and sanctions against debt collection agencies found guilty of widespread FDCPA violations.

3. Public awareness campaigns and consumer advocacy efforts that expose debt collectors' illegal practices, leading to increased scrutiny and accountability within the industry.

Understanding the penalties associated with FDCPA violations reinforces the importance of debt collectors adhering to the regulations outlined in the law. By asserting your rights and reporting violations, you contribute to the enforcement of the FDCPA and the protection of consumers from unfair and abusive debt collection practices.

In the next chapter, we will shift our focus to the role of consumer protection laws in safeguarding consumers' rights and the fines for non-compliance with key consumer protection acts.

Chapter 6: Consumer Protection Laws and Fines for Non-Compliance

The Role of Consumer Protection Laws:

Consumer protection laws play a crucial role in safeguarding the rights and interests of consumers. These laws establish guidelines and regulations that businesses must follow to ensure fair and ethical practices. In this chapter, we will explore key consumer protection laws and the fines associated with non-compliance.

1. The Fair Credit Reporting Act (FCRA):

The FCRA regulates the collection, dissemination, and use of consumer credit information. It ensures the accuracy and privacy of credit reports and provides consumers with rights to dispute and correct inaccurate information. Non-compliance with the FCRA can result in significant fines and penalties.

- Fines for FCRA Violations: Violations of the FCRA can lead to fines imposed by regulatory agencies, such as the Consumer Financial Protection Bureau (CFPB). The specific fines depend on the severity of the violation and can range from thousands to millions of dollars.

2. The Fair Debt Collection Practices Act (FDCPA):

The FDCPA establishes rules and limitations for debt collectors when attempting to collect debts from consumers. It aims to prevent abusive and deceptive practices and protect consumers' rights during the debt collection process.

- Fines for FDCPA Violations: Violations of the FDCPA can result in regulatory enforcement actions and lawsuits. Debt collectors found guilty of FDCPA violations may be subject to civil penalties, which can range from hundreds to thousands of dollars per violation.

3. The Federal Trade Commission Act (FTCA):

The FTCA empowers the Federal Trade Commission (FTC) to regulate and enforce various consumer protection laws. It prohibits unfair and deceptive acts or practices in commerce.

- Fines for FTCA Violations: Violations of the FTCA can lead to significant fines imposed by the FTC. The fines vary depending on the nature of the violation, the size of the business involved, and other relevant factors.

4. The Consumer Financial Protection Act (CFPA):

The CFPA grants the Consumer Financial Protection Bureau (CFPB) the authority to enforce federal consumer financial laws. It focuses on protecting consumers from unfair, deceptive, or abusive practices in the financial industry.

- Fines for CFPA Violations: The CFPB has the power to impose fines on individuals or entities that violate consumer financial protection laws. The fines can be substantial, ranging from thousands to millions of dollars.

Understanding the fines associated with non-compliance serves as a strong deterrent for businesses, encouraging them to comply with consumer protection laws and prioritize consumer welfare. The fines act as a means of punishment and reinforce the importance of adhering to these regulations.

In the next section, we will explore the role and operations of the Consumer Financial Protection Bureau (CFPB) and how consumers can leverage its resources to assist them in credit disputes and complaints against financial institutions.

Chapter 7: The Consumer Financial Protection Bureau (CFPB) and Its Role in Assisting Consumers

Introduction to the Consumer Financial Protection Bureau (CFPB):

The Consumer Financial Protection Bureau (CFPB) is a federal agency responsible for protecting consumers in the financial marketplace. Established under the Dodd-Frank Wall Street Reform and Consumer Protection Act, the CFPB's primary mission is to ensure fair treatment, transparency, and accountability for consumers when dealing with financial products and services.

Understanding the Operations of the CFPB:

The CFPB operates through various mechanisms to fulfill its mission of consumer protection. Here are some key aspects of its operations:

1. **Rulemaking and Enforcement:**

The CFPB has the authority to issue regulations and rules that govern the practices of financial institutions.

These rules are designed to protect consumers from unfair, deceptive, or abusive practices. The CFPB also enforces these rules and takes action against institutions that violate consumer protection laws.

2. **Consumer Complaint Database:**

The CFPB maintains a Consumer Complaint Database where consumers can submit complaints regarding financial products and services. This database serves as a valuable resource for consumers to voice their concerns and seek resolution for their issues. It also helps the CFPB identify patterns of misconduct and take appropriate actions.

3. **Education and Resources:**

The CFPB provides educational materials and resources to empower consumers with knowledge about their rights and responsibilities in the financial marketplace. Through its website, publications, and consumer guides, the CFPB aims to improve financial literacy and help consumers make informed decisions.

4. **Supervision and Examination:**

The CFPB has supervisory authority over certain financial institutions, including banks, credit unions, and mortgage servicers. It conducts examinations to ensure compliance with consumer protection laws and regulations. These examinations help identify potential violations and promote a fair and transparent financial marketplace.

5. **Collaboration with Other Agencies:**

The CFPB collaborates with other federal, state, and local agencies to coordinate efforts in protecting consumers. This collaboration fosters a comprehensive approach to consumer protection and enhances the effectiveness of regulatory actions.

How Consumers Can Utilize the CFPB for Disputes and Complaints:

If you encounter issues with financial products or services, the CFPB can be a valuable resource to assist you. Here's how you can utilize the CFPB:

1. **File a Complaint:**

If you have a complaint against a financial institution, you can submit it to the CFPB through their website or by contacting their consumer hotline. Provide detailed information about the issue and any supporting documentation. The CFPB will review your complaint and work to facilitate a resolution.

2. **Access Consumer Tools and Resources:**

Explore the CFPB's website to access consumer tools, guides, and resources. These resources can help you understand your rights, navigate financial decisions, and take proactive steps to protect yourself.

3. **Stay Informed:**

Keep up-to-date with the latest news and announcements from the CFPB. They regularly release reports, studies, and guidance that can help you make informed financial choices and stay aware of emerging consumer protection issues.

4. **Report Suspected Scams or Fraud:**

If you come across suspected scams or fraudulent activities, report them to the CFPB. They investigate these reports and take appropriate action to protect consumers from fraudulent practices.

By utilizing the resources and services provided by the CFPB, consumers can seek assistance, resolve disputes, and contribute to the overall improvement of the financial marketplace.

In the next chapter, we will delve into how credit reporting agencies violate the Privacy Act and examine the statements made by Congress regarding credit reporting agencies. We will also explore the relevant laws that govern their operations.

Chapter 8: Violations of the Privacy Act by Credit Reporting Agencies

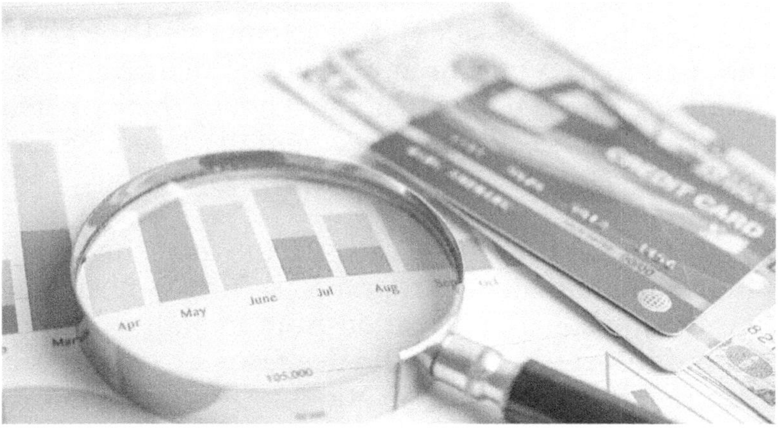

Understanding the Privacy Act and Its Relevance to Credit Reporting:

The Privacy Act is a federal law that regulates the collection, use, and dissemination of personal information by federal agencies. While credit reporting agencies are not federal agencies, their operations involve handling and reporting personal information, which can sometimes lead to violations of the Privacy Act. In this chapter, we will explore how credit reporting agencies may violate the Privacy Act and the implications of such violations.

1. Types of Privacy Act Violations:

a) Unauthorized Disclosure: Credit reporting agencies may disclose personal information to unauthorized entities or individuals without the consumer's consent or a lawful basis for disclosure.

b) Inaccurate Information Handling: Mishandling or misreporting personal information can lead to Privacy

Act violations. This includes inaccurately linking individuals to accounts or reporting inaccurate financial data.

c) Failure to Provide Notice: Credit reporting agencies are required to inform individuals of their rights under the Privacy Act, including how their personal information is collected, used, and disclosed. Failure to provide adequate notice can result in violations.

d) Inadequate Safeguards: Credit reporting agencies must implement appropriate security measures to protect personal information from unauthorized access or disclosure. Insufficient safeguards or data breaches can lead to Privacy Act violations.

2. Congressional Statements on Credit Reporting Agencies: 15 U.S. Code §1681 Congressional findings.

Congress has expressed concerns about credit reporting agencies' handling of personal information and the potential for Privacy Act violations. Statements made by Congress regarding credit reporting agencies include:

a) The Fair and Accurate Credit Transactions Act (FACTA): This legislation was enacted to enhance consumer rights and improve the accuracy of credit reporting. It highlights the importance of protecting consumer privacy and provides mechanisms for consumers to dispute inaccuracies in their credit reports.

b) Congressional Hearings and Investigations: Congress has conducted hearings and investigations to scrutinize credit reporting agencies' practices and address concerns related to consumer privacy. These proceedings have shed light on potential violations and the need for stronger safeguards.

3. Relevant Laws Governing Credit Reporting Agencies:

a) Fair Credit Reporting Act (FCRA): The FCRA establishes guidelines for credit reporting agencies' operations and protects consumer privacy rights. It outlines requirements for handling and reporting consumer information, including dispute resolution procedures and the removal of inaccurate or outdated information.

b) Gramm-Leach-Bliley Act (GLBA): The GLBA requires financial institutions, including credit reporting agencies, to implement safeguards to protect the privacy and security of consumer information. It mandates the development and maintenance of privacy policies and practices.

Consequences of Privacy Act Violations:

When credit reporting agencies violate the Privacy Act, they may face legal consequences and sanctions. These can include:

a) Lawsuits and Legal Action: Individuals whose privacy rights have been violated can pursue legal action against credit reporting agencies. This can result in financial settlements or court judgments against the agencies.

b) Regulatory Actions: Regulatory bodies, such as the Consumer Financial Protection Bureau (CFPB) or the Federal Trade Commission (FTC), can take enforcement actions against credit reporting agencies for Privacy Act violations. These actions may involve fines, penalties, and mandated corrective actions.

c) Reputational Damage: Privacy Act violations can tarnish the reputation of credit reporting agencies, leading to a loss of consumer trust and credibility. This can have long-term consequences for their business operations and relationships with creditors.

It is crucial for credit reporting agencies to comply with the Privacy Act and ensure the proper handling and protection of consumers' personal information. By holding them accountable for any violations, consumers can protect their privacy rights and contribute to the overall improvement of data privacy practices within the credit reporting industry.

In the next chapter, we will explore the importance of opting out of marketing and solicitation and provide step-by-step instructions on how consumers can exercise their right to opt out

. We will also discuss why this is significant for safeguarding privacy and reducing unwanted offers.

Chapter 9: Opting Out of Marketing and Solicitation for Privacy Protection

Introduction to Opting Out:

In today's digital age, consumers are often bombarded with marketing messages and solicitations, both online and offline. However, individuals have the right to protect their privacy and limit unwanted communications. In this chapter, we will explore the importance of opting out of marketing and solicitation and provide step-by-step instructions on how consumers can exercise their right to opt out.

1. **Understanding the Importance of Opting Out:**

a) Privacy Protection: Opting out helps protect your personal information from being shared with third-party marketers and organizations. By limiting the dissemination of your data, you reduce the risk of receiving unsolicited marketing materials and potential privacy breaches.

b) Reduced Unwanted Offers: Opting out of marketing communications ensures that you only receive promotional materials from companies and organizations you have chosen to engage with. This helps declutter your mailbox, email inbox, and phone calls, making it easier to focus on relevant and desired information.

c) Enhanced Data Security: Opting out minimizes the exposure of your personal information to unauthorized parties, reducing the chances of your data falling into the wrong hands. This contributes to better overall data security and mitigates the risks of identity theft or fraud.

2. Opting Out Methods and Techniques:

a) Direct Marketing Opt-Out: Many companies provide opt-out options for their marketing communications. This includes email newsletters, promotional offers, and physical mailings. Look for opt-out links or instructions in the communications you receive, and follow the provided steps to unsubscribe or opt out.

b) National Do Not Call Registry: In many countries, including the United States, there are national registries that allow you to opt out of receiving telemarketing calls. Register your phone number(s) on these lists to reduce unwanted solicitation calls.

c) Opt-Out of Credit Offers: To reduce credit card and loan offers, you can opt out through the official website or toll-free number provided by credit reporting agencies. This prevents your credit information from being shared with potential creditors for promotional purposes.

d) Online Advertising Opt-Out: Online behavioral advertising can be managed by opting out of targeted advertising networks. Visit the websites of advertising industry associations or use online tools provided by browsers to customize your advertising preferences and opt out of personalized ads.

3. Benefits and Considerations:

a) Privacy Enhancement: Opting out empowers you to regain control over your personal information, allowing you to manage how it is used and shared.

b) Time and Effort: While opting out may require some initial time and effort to update your preferences and contact various organizations, it can save you time and frustration in the long run by reducing unwanted communications.

c) Relevance of Opt-Out Periods: Note that opt-out periods may vary, and it may take some time for your preferences to be fully implemented across all platforms and organizations. Be patient and monitor your communications to ensure opt-out effectiveness.

d) Exceptions and Account Management: Keep in mind that certain communications, such as transactional messages or account-related notifications, may still be sent even if you opt out of marketing communications. Review and manage your preferences accordingly.

By actively opting out of marketing and solicitation, you assert control over your personal information and reduce unwanted communications. This proactive approach contributes to a more privacy-conscious and focused engagement with businesses and organizations.

Opting out of certain companies and their marketing communications can be a useful step for privacy protection and reducing unwanted solicitations. While individual preferences may vary, here are some important companies and their opt-out websites that you may consider:

1. Direct Marketing Association (DMA): The DMA provides a service called DMAchoice, which allows you to opt out of direct mail and email marketing from various companies. Visit their website at www.dmachoice.org to manage your preferences.

2. National Do Not Call Registry: The National Do Not Call Registry allows you to register your phone number to opt out of telemarketing calls. To add your phone number to the registry or check your registration status, visit www.donotcall.gov.

3. Credit Reporting Agencies: Opting out of pre-screened credit offers can help reduce unwanted credit card and loan solicitations. You can opt out by visiting the websites of the three major credit reporting agencies:

Equifax: www.equifax.com/personal/credit-report-services/credit-freeze

Experian: www.experian.com/freeze/center.html

TransUnion: www.transunion.com/credit-help

4. Online Advertising Networks: Online advertising networks track your browsing activity to personalize ads. You can opt out of targeted advertising through the following websites:

- Network Advertising Initiative (NAI):

  www.networkadvertising.org/choices

- Digital Advertising Alliance (DAA):

  www.aboutads.info/choices

5. Data Brokers: Data brokers collect and sell personal information. Some prominent data brokers offer opt-out options:

- Acxiom:

  www.acxiom.com/about-us/privacy/opt-out

- Opt-Out IQ: www.optoutiq.com

- Whitepages:

  www.whitepages.com/suppression_requests

6. Specific Service Providers: Many service providers offer opt-out options for their own marketing communications. Examples include:

- Google: www.google.com/ads/preferences
- Facebook: Visit the "Settings & Privacy" section of your Facebook account to manage ad preferences.
- Amazon: www.amazon.com/adprefs

Major data collection companies that provide information to credit bureaus and their opt-out websites:

1. LexisNexis: LexisNexis is a leading provider of consumer data for various purposes, including credit reporting. You can request to opt out of LexisNexis data by visiting their opt-out website:

www.lexisnexis.com/privacy/opt-out.

5. Innovis: Innovis is a consumer credit reporting agency that collects and provides information to lenders and creditors. To opt out of Innovis, visit their website at

www.innovis.com/creditReport/optOut.

6. SageStream (formerly known as ID Analytics): SageStream is a consumer reporting agency that provides credit-related information to lenders and other businesses. You can opt out of SageStream by visiting their website:

www.sagestreamllc.com/privacy-policy/consumer-information.

7. ChexSystems: ChexSystems is a specialty consumer reporting agency that focuses on

banking and checking account history. To opt out of ChexSystems, you can send a request by mail. Visit their website for instructions:

www.chexsystems.com/web/chexsystems/consumer debit/optout.

8. ARS (Advanced Resolution Services): ARS is a consumer reporting agency that provides information related to debt collections. To opt out of ARS, you can submit a request through their opt-out website:

www.advancedresolutionservices.com/opt-out.

It's important to note that the opt-out processes and effectiveness may vary among these companies. Some may require you to provide specific identification information, follow additional steps, or submit requests via mail. Take the time to carefully review the opt-out instructions on each company's website for accurate and up-to-date information.

Opting out from these data collection companies can help limit the sharing of your information with credit bureaus and other entities. However, it's worth noting that these opt-outs may not completely eliminate all data sharing or collection activities, as there may be other sources and methods used by credit bureaus and data collectors.

Regularly reviewing your privacy settings, monitoring your credit reports, and staying informed about your rights can help maintain control over your personal information and credit reporting activities.

In the next chapter, we will discuss effective strategies for rebuilding your credit score. We will explore specific tradelines that can help boost your credit score without resorting to purchasing trade lines, providing you with practical steps to improve your creditworthiness.

Chapter 10: Rebuilding Your Credit Score

Understanding Credit Score Basics:

Your credit score is a numerical representation of your creditworthiness and plays a significant role in determining your access to credit and favorable interest rates. If you've faced financial challenges or made credit mistakes in the past, it's essential to know that it's never too late to start rebuilding your credit score. In this chapter, we will explore effective strategies for rebuilding your credit score and regaining financial stability.

1. Assessing Your Current Credit Situation:

a) Obtaining Your Credit Reports: Start by obtaining copies of your credit reports from the major credit bureaus—Equifax, Experian, and TransUnion. Review the reports thoroughly to understand your current credit standing, including any negative or derogatory information.

b) Identifying Negative Items: Pay close attention to negative items such as late payments, collections, or charge-offs. These items have a significant impact on your credit score and should be addressed during the rebuilding process.

2. **Disputing Inaccurate or Outdated Information:**

a) Utilizing the Fair Credit Reporting Act (FCRA): The FCRA grants you the right to dispute inaccurate or outdated information on your credit reports. Follow the step-by-step guide provided in Chapter 3 to initiate a dispute with the credit bureaus and request the removal of any erroneous items.

b) Providing Supporting Documentation: When disputing items, gather supporting documentation that substantiates your claim of inaccuracies. This may include payment receipts, correspondence, or any other relevant information that proves the item is incorrect.

3. **Establishing Positive Payment History:**

a) Timely Payment of Current Debts: One of the most crucial factors in rebuilding your credit score is consistently making on-time payments for your current debts. Set up automatic payments or reminders to ensure you never miss a payment.

b) Negotiating Payment Plans: If you're struggling to make payments, contact your creditors to discuss possible payment arrangements or hardship programs. Establishing a payment plan demonstrates your commitment to resolving your debts and can help improve your creditworthiness.

4. Adding Positive Tradelines to Your Credit Report:

a) Authorized User Status: Ask a trusted family member or friend with good credit to add you as an authorized user on their credit card account. Their positive payment history and credit utilization will be reflected on your credit report, potentially boosting your credit score.

b) Secured Credit Cards: Consider opening a secured credit card, which requires a cash deposit as collateral. Use the card responsibly, making timely payments and keeping your credit utilization low. Over time, this can help rebuild your credit score.

c) Credit Builder Loans: Some financial institutions offer credit builder loans specifically designed to help individuals rebuild their credit. These loans work by holding the loan funds in an account while you make regular payments, establishing a positive payment history.

5. Monitoring Your Progress:

a) Regularly Check Your Credit Reports: Monitor your credit reports regularly to track the progress of your credit rebuilding efforts. Look for improvements in your credit score and the removal of any disputed or negative items.

b) Utilize Credit Monitoring Services: Consider enrolling in credit monitoring services that provide real-time updates and alerts about changes to your credit reports. These services can help you stay informed and take immediate action if any new issues arise.

Remember, rebuilding your credit score takes time and patience. By implementing these strategies and maintaining responsible credit habits, you can gradually improve your creditworthiness and regain financial stability.

In the final chapter, we will conclude our guide by summarizing the key concepts covered throughout the book and providing final words of advice to help you on your journey to credit success.

Chapter 11: Taking Control of Your Financial Future

Congratulations on completing the comprehensive guide to fixing your credit and boosting your credit score! Now that you have gained a deeper understanding of credit bureaus, consumer protection laws, and credit repair strategies, it's time to take control of your financial future. In this final chapter, we will explore additional steps you can take to maintain and improve your credit over the long term.

1. **Budgeting and Financial Planning:**

- Create a realistic budget that aligns with your income and expenses. Track your spending and make necessary adjustments to ensure you live within your means.

- Prioritize saving and build an emergency fund to protect yourself from unexpected financial setbacks.
- Consider seeking professional financial advice to develop a comprehensive financial plan tailored to your goals and circumstances.

2. **Responsible Credit Card Usage:**

- Use credit cards responsibly by charging only what you can afford to pay off in full each month. Avoid carrying high balances or accumulating excessive debt.

- Pay your credit card bills on time to maintain a positive payment history and avoid late fees.

- Monitor your credit card statements regularly for any unauthorized charges or errors.

3. **Debt Management Strategies:**

- If you have existing debts, develop a debt repayment plan. Prioritize paying off high-interest debts first while making minimum payments on other debts.

- Consider debt consolidation options to simplify your repayment process and potentially lower your interest rates.

- Avoid taking on new debts unless necessary and carefully evaluate the terms and conditions before entering into any financial agreements.

4. Regular Credit Monitoring:

- Continue monitoring your credit reports on a regular basis. Check for any new inaccuracies, fraudulent accounts, or suspicious activities.

- Stay vigilant about identity theft by reviewing your credit reports, monitoring bank accounts, and protecting your personal information. I recommend IDENITY IQ Start for $1.00 for 7 days then regular billing

https://member.identityiq.com/securepreferred.aspx?offercode=431277CM start for 1.00

5. Building Positive Financial Habits:

- Cultivate healthy financial habits such as saving a portion of your income, living within your means, and avoiding unnecessary expenses.

- Educate yourself about personal finance topics, such as investing, retirement planning, and building wealth. Knowledge empowers you to make informed financial decisions.

6. Utilizing Additional Resources:

- Stay informed about updates in credit laws, consumer rights, and financial regulations. Keep up with changes that may impact your credit or personal finances.
- Take advantage of online resources, financial literacy programs, and educational materials provided by reputable organizations and government agencies.

Remember, maintaining good credit and financial well-being is an ongoing process. It requires discipline, commitment, and a proactive approach to managing your finances. By applying the knowledge and strategies outlined in this book, you have taken a significant step toward improving your credit and securing a brighter financial future.

As you embark on your journey to financial success, keep your goals in mind, stay motivated, and adapt your strategies as needed. You have the power to shape your financial destiny and build a solid foundation for a prosperous life. Good luck on your continued credit repair and financial journey!

Chapter 12: Conclusion

Recap of Key Concepts:

Throughout this book, we have delved into the intricate world of credit bureaus, credit reports, and the laws that protect consumers. Let's recap the key concepts covered and the steps you can take to fix your credit and boost your credit score.

1. Importance of Credit:

- Understanding the impact of credit on your financial life, including loan approvals, interest rates, and rental applications.

- Recognizing the significance of credit reports and credit scores in assessing your creditworthiness.

2. Discharging Student Loan Debt Using the ACTS or LAWS of the United States:

- Exploring options for discharging student loan debt under applicable laws.

- Providing a step-by-step guide to navigating the process and seeking relief.

3. Disputing Items on Your Credit Report with the FCRA:

- Understanding the Fair Credit Reporting Act (FCRA) and your rights as a consumer.

- Step-by-step instructions for disputing inaccurate or outdated information on your credit report.

4. Penalties for Violating the FCRA:

- Highlighting the consequences of non-compliance with the FCRA.

- Examining real-life cases and their outcomes to emphasize the importance of following the law.

5. Dealing with Debt Collectors Using the FDCPA:

- Familiarizing yourself with the Fair Debt Collection Practices Act (FDCPA) and its provisions.

- Equipping you with the knowledge to handle debt collectors and exercise your consumer rights.

6. Penalties for Violating the FDCPA:

- Understanding the severe penalties for willful non-compliance with the FDCPA.

- Exploring notable cases and their legal ramifications as a deterrent.

7. Consumer Protection Laws and Their Importance:

- Recognizing the role of consumer protection laws in safeguarding consumer rights.

- Understanding the fines and penalties associated with non-compliance.

8. Understanding the Consumer Financial Protection Bureau (CFPB):

- Introducing the CFPB and its mission to protect consumers in the financial marketplace.

- Guiding you on how to file a complaint and seek assistance in credit disputes.

9. Privacy Act Violations by Credit Reporting Agencies:

- Highlighting instances of Privacy Act violations by credit reporting agencies.

- Citing relevant legislation and congressional statements regarding credit reporting agencies.

10. Opting Out of Marketing and Solicitation:

- Explaining the importance of opting out to protect your privacy and reduce unwanted offers.

- Providing step-by-step instructions for opting out through various channels.

11. Rebuilding Your Credit Score:

- Emphasizing the significance of assessing your current credit situation and disputing inaccuracies.

- Offering strategies to establish positive payment history and add positive tradelines to improve your creditworthiness.

Final Words of Advice:

As you embark on your journey to fix your credit and boost your credit score, keep the following advice in mind:

1. Patience and Persistence: Rebuilding your credit takes time and dedication. Be patient and persistent in implementing the strategies outlined in this book.

2. Stay Informed: Continue educating yourself about credit laws, consumer rights, and financial best practices. Knowledge is power when it comes to managing your credit effectively.

3. Responsible Credit Habits: Practice responsible credit habits moving forward. Make timely payments, keep credit utilization low, and avoid taking on excessive debt.

4. Regular Monitoring: Monitor your credit reports regularly to ensure accuracy and detect any signs of identity theft or fraud. Utilize credit monitoring services for added peace of mind.

5. Seek Professional Help if Needed: If you find the credit repair process overwhelming or encounter complex issues, consider consulting with a reputable credit counseling agency or credit repair professional for guidance.

Your credit journey is unique, and it requires ongoing effort to maintain a healthy credit profile. By utilizing the knowledge and tools provided in this

Bonus #1 Resources to assist in your Journey:

Here is a list of websites and resources that consumers can utilize to assist them in fixing their credit reports and building their credit scores at no cost:

1. AnnualCreditReport.com: This website allows consumers to request free credit reports from each of the three major credit bureaus (Equifax, Experian, and TransUnion) once every 12 months.

2. Credit Karma (creditkarma.com): Credit Karma provides free access to credit reports and credit scores from TransUnion and Equifax. It also offers tools and educational resources to help consumers understand and monitor their credit.

3. Experian Boost (experian.com/boost): Experian Boost allows consumers to add positive payment history from their utility bills and phone bills to their Experian credit report, potentially boosting their credit scores.

4. Discover Credit Scorecard (creditscorecard.com): Discover offers a free service that provides consumers with their FICO credit score based on Experian credit report data. It also offers credit monitoring and helpful credit education resources.

5. MyFICO Forums (ficoforums.myfico.com): MyFICO Forums are an online community where consumers can connect with others to discuss credit-related topics, share experiences, and learn from each other.

6. Federal Trade Commission (FTC) - Credit and Loans (ftc.gov/credit-and-loans): The FTC's website provides valuable information and resources on credit

and loans, including steps to dispute errors on credit reports, protecting against identity theft, and understanding consumer rights.

7. Consumer Financial Protection Bureau (CFPB) - Credit Reports and Scores (consumerfinance.gov/credit-reports-and-scores): The CFPB offers educational resources and tools to help consumers understand credit reports, dispute errors, and improve their credit scores.

8. National Foundation for Credit Counseling (NFCC) (nfcc.org): NFCC is a nonprofit organization that provides free or low-cost credit counseling services. Consumers can find credit counseling agencies in their area through their website.

9. Federal Student Aid (studentaid.gov): For individuals with student loans, this U.S. Department of Education website provides resources and information on loan repayment options, loan consolidation, and loan forgiveness programs.

10. IdentityTheft.gov: This website, managed by the FTC, provides step-by-step guidance to help individuals report and recover from identity theft. It offers tools for disputing fraudulent accounts and creating a personalized recovery plan.

11. CreditCards.com: CreditCards.com offers free resources and tools to help consumers understand credit cards, compare offers, and make informed decisions about credit card usage.

12. bankrate.com: Bankrate.com provides financial calculators, articles, and guides to help consumers make informed financial decisions, including tips on improving credit scores and managing debt.

Remember to exercise caution and verify the credibility of any websites or services before providing personal information or utilizing their resources. These resources can serve as valuable tools for consumers seeking to improve their credit profiles and financial well-being.

Bonus #2 10 Positive trade line-building solutions for credit building

1. Secured Credit Cards: Obtain a secured credit card by making a cash deposit as collateral. Use the card responsibly, making timely payments, to demonstrate good credit management.

2. Authorized User Accounts: Ask a trusted family member or friend with a well-managed credit card to add you as an authorized user. Their positive payment history will reflect on your credit report.

3. Credit Builder Loans: Consider applying for a credit builder loan, where you make regular payments into a savings account. Once the loan is repaid, you receive the funds along with an improved credit history.

4. Peer-to-Peer Lending: Utilize peer-to-peer lending platforms that allow individuals to lend and borrow money directly. Making on-time payments on these loans can positively impact your credit score.

5. Rent Reporting Services: Enroll in rent reporting services that report your rental payments to credit bureaus. This can help build a positive payment history for non-traditional credit users.

6. Credit Builder Accounts: Some financial institutions offer credit builder accounts that allow you to save money while simultaneously building credit. These accounts are specifically designed to help improve credit scores.

7. Retail Store Credit Cards: Apply for retail store credit cards and use them responsibly. Make small

purchases and pay off the balances in full each month to demonstrate creditworthiness.

8. Credit Union Memberships: Join a credit union and take advantage of their credit-building products, such as credit builder loans and secured credit cards, which may offer favorable terms.

9. Peer-to-Peer Rental Reporting: Use peer-to-peer rental reporting services that report your on-time rent payments to credit bureaus. This can help establish a positive payment history.

10. Alternative Credit Scoring Models: Explore alternative credit scoring models, such as Experian's Boost and UltraFICO, which consider additional factors like utility bill payments and savings patterns to determine creditworthiness.

Remember to research and compare the terms, fees, and benefits of each option before making any decisions. Additionally, maintaining responsible credit habits, such as making payments on time, keeping credit card balances low, and monitoring your credit reports, will also contribute to a positive credit-building journey.

Note: For specific websites and platforms related to these options, you can conduct a search online or refer to reputable financial websites that provide information and reviews on credit-building services.

companies and their website addresses:

Secured Credit Card Companies:

1. Capital One Secured Mastercard: capitalone.com/credit-cards/secured-mastercard/

2. Discover it® Secured Credit Card: discover.com/credit-cards/secured/

3. Citi® Secured Mastercard®: citi.com/credit-cards/credit-card-details/citi.action?ID=citi-secured-credit-card

4. OpenSky® Secured Visa® Credit Card: openskycc.com/

5. Applied Bank® Secured Visa® Gold Preferred® Credit Card: appliedbank.com/personal/personal-credit-cards

Authorized User Options:

1. https://tradelinesupply.com/how-to-choose-a-tradeline/

2. https://superiortradelines.com/

3. https://www.callcreditpro.com/

5. https://prioritytradelines.com/

Credit Builder Loans:

1. Self (formerly Self Lender): self.inc/

2. Credit Strong: creditstrong.com/

3. MoneyLion Credit Builder Plus: moneylion.com/credit-builder-plus

4. OneMain Financial: onemainfinancial.com/

5. Credit Builder by Republic Bank: rbcbank.com/personal/borrowing/credit-builder

Peer-to-Peer Lending (Not for Very Bad Credit)

1. LendingClub: lendingclub.com/
2. Prosper: prosper.com/

4. Upstart: upstart.com/

5. Peerform: peerform.com/

5. Funding Circle: fundingcircle.com/

Rent Reporting Services:

1. RentTrack: renttrack.com/

2. Rental Kharma: rentalkharma.com/

3. PayYourRent: payyourrent.com/

4. LevelCredit: levelcredit.com/

5. RentReporters: rentreporters.com/

Credit Builder Accounts:

1. Chime Credit Builder Visa® Secured Credit Card: chime.com/

2. Aspiration Spend & Save: aspiration.com/

3. Varo Bank Account with Credit Builder: varomoney.com/

4. Step Mobile Banking with Fee-Free Overdraft: step.com/

5. Current Premium Banking: current.com/

Retail Store Cards for People with Poor Credit:

1. Fingerhut Credit Account: fingerhut.com/

2. Capital One Walmart Rewards® Card: walmart.capitalone.com/

3. Kohl's Card: kohls.com/

4. JCPenney Credit Card: jcpcreditcard.com/

5. Target REDcard™: target.com/redcard/

Credit Union Memberships for People with Poor Credit:

1. Navy Federal Credit Union: navyfederal.org/

2. PenFed Credit Union: penfed.org/
3. Alliant Credit Union: alliantcreditunion.org/

4. Golden 1 Credit Union: golden1.com/

5. Digital Federal Credit Union (DCU): dcu.org/

Peer-to-Peer Rental Reporting:

1. RentReporters: rentreporters.com/

2. Rental Kharma: rentalkharma.com/

3. RentTrack: renttrack.com/

Alternative Credit Scoring Models:

1. Experian Boost: experian.com/credit-services/experian-boost.html

2. UltraFICO™: fico.com/ultrafico

3. eCredable Lift: ecredable.com/lift

4. PRBC: prbc.com/

5. Payment Reporting Builds Credit (PRBC): prbc.com/

Please note that availability and terms may vary, so it's essential to visit each website and review the specific details and requirements of each company before applying or using their services.

Bonus #3 ENFORCEMENT Templates

STEP1 CREDIT DISPUTE LETTER

Note: (Include ID, Utility bill or proof of address and proof of social security number example Tax Document, SS Card)

Certified Mail #. 3638 8383 0303 3030
[Your Name]
[Your Address]
[City, State, ZIP Code]
[Date]

[Credit Bureau Name]
[Credit Bureau Address]
[City, State, ZIP Code]

Credit Report #

Dispute of Inaccurate Information on Credit Report - Violation of Fair Credit Reporting Act (FCRA)

Dear [Credit Bureau Name],

I am writing to formally dispute the following inaccurate information appearing on my credit report, as mandated by the Fair Credit Reporting Act (FCRA). I demand immediate removal of these items as they are in violation of my rights under the FCRA, and failure to comply will result in severe consequences.

1. [Inaccurate Account Information]

   - Account Name: [Incorrect Account Name]
   - Account Number: [Incorrect Account Number]
   - Date Reported: [Date of Incorrect Reporting]

- Description of Inaccuracy: [Describe the specific error or inaccuracy]

2. [Inaccurate Account Information]

- Account Name: [Incorrect Account Name]
- Account Number: [Incorrect Account Number]
- Date Reported: [Date of Incorrect Reporting]
- Description of Inaccuracy: [Describe the specific error or inaccuracy]

Under Section 611 of the FCRA, I am exercising my right to dispute these inaccuracies and demanding a thorough investigation within the legally mandated timeframe of 30 days. The FCRA requires credit bureaus to promptly investigate disputed items and correct any information found to be inaccurate, incomplete, or unverifiable.

I want to emphasize that any willful non-compliance with the FCRA may result in serious legal consequences, including but not limited to:

1. Civil Liability: The FCRA provides individuals who have suffered harm due to non-compliance with the right to seek legal recourse. Failure to remove inaccurate items could result in legal action seeking damages for the harm caused by the violations.

2. Statutory Damages: The FCRA allows for the recovery of statutory damages in cases of willful non-compliance, with penalties ranging from $100 to $1,000 per violation, depending on the severity of the violation.
3. Injunctive Relief: Individuals may also seek injunctive relief, requesting a court order to enforce compliance with the FCRA and ensure the removal of inaccurate information.

It is imperative that you understand the gravity of the situation and take immediate action to rectify these inaccuracies. Any delay or failure to comply will be viewed as a willful violation of the FCRA, and I will not hesitate to take legal action to protect my rights and seek the appropriate remedies available under the law.

I expect to receive written confirmation of the investigation process and a detailed report of the actions taken to resolve these disputes within the specified timeframe. Additionally, I request that you inform me of any notifications sent to the data furnishers regarding the removal of the inaccurate information from their records.

Your cooperation in this matter is expected, and I trust that you will act in accordance with the FCRA and resolve these disputes promptly. Failure to do so will leave me no choice but to pursue legal remedies to enforce my rights.

Thank you for your immediate attention to this matter.

Sincerely,

[Your Name]

[Your Contact Information: Phone Number and Email Address]
Enclosures:
- Copy of Credit Report
Supporting Documentation

NOTE: MAILING ADDRESS
Here are the dispute mailing addresses for Equifax, TransUnion, and Experian:

Equifax Information Services LLC
P.O. Box 740256
Atlanta, GA 30374-0256

TransUnion LLC
Consumer Dispute Center
P.O. Box 2000
Chester, PA 19016

Experian
P.O. Box 4500
Allen, TX 75013

When sending your dispute documents, it is recommended to use certified mail with a return receipt requested. This will provide proof of delivery and ensure that someone at the credit bureau signs for and receives the documents.

Mailing addresses and the names of the CEOs for Equifax, TransUnion, and Experian in the USA:

Equifax Inc.
Attn: Mark W. Begor (CEO)
1550 Peachtree Street NW
Atlanta, GA 30309

TransUnion LLC
Attn: Christopher A. Cartwright (CEO)
555 West Adams Street
Chicago, IL 60661

Experian Information Solutions Inc.
Attn: Craig Boundy (CEO)
475 Anton Boulevard
Costa Mesa, CA 92626

Please note that while these addresses are for their respective headquarters, it's important to consult with legal professionals or follow proper legal procedures for any legal actions or notices of intent to sue.

STEP 2 CREDIT DISPUTE LETTER

Note: (Include ID, Utility bill or proof of address and proof of social security number example Tax Document, SS Card)

Certified Mail #. 3638 8383 0303 3030 (signed PS 3800 or Electronic Signature check on PS 3800)
[Your Name]
[Your Address]
[City, State, ZIP Code]
[Date]

[Credit Bureau Name]
[Credit Bureau Address]
[City, State, ZIP Code]

Credit Report #

Second Notice Of Dispute- Violation of Fair Credit Reporting Act and Privacy Act of 1974

Dear [Credit Bureau Name],

I am writing to follow up on my previous dispute letter dated [Date] regarding the inaccurate information on my credit report. It has come to my attention that the credit reporting agencies, including [Credit Bureau Name], have not only violated the Fair Credit Reporting Act (FCRA) but also the Privacy Act of 1974 (5 U.S. Code § 552a). The following disputes below are still reporting inaccurately on my credit disclosure causing me harm and damages.

1. [Inaccurate Account Information]

   - Account Name: [Incorrect Account Name]
   - Account Number: [Incorrect Account Number]

- Date Reported: [Date of Incorrect Reporting]
- Description of Inaccuracy: [Describe the specific error or inaccuracy]

3. [Inaccurate Account Information]

- Account Name: [Incorrect Account Name]
- Account Number: [Incorrect Account Number]
- Date Reported: [Date of Incorrect Reporting]
- Description of Inaccuracy: [Describe the specific error or inaccuracy]

Under the Privacy Act of 1974, I wish to bring to your attention the following violations:

1. Disclosure of Records: Section 552a(b) of the Privacy Act prohibits the disclosure of any record contained in a system of records without the prior written consent of the individual to whom the record pertains, unless permitted by law. The information contained in my credit report constitutes a record under the Privacy Act, and its disclosure without my prior written consent is a direct violation of this provision.

2. Disclosure to Consumer Reporting Agencies: Section 552a(b)(12) of the Privacy Act allows disclosure of records to consumer reporting agencies only with the prior written request or consent of the individual to whom the record pertains. It has come to my attention that such prior written consent was not obtained before disclosing my information to the consumer reporting agencies.

3. Section 3711(e) of Title 31 Violation: Section 3711(e) of Title 31 permits the disclosure of information from a system of records to a consumer reporting agency only if satisfactory assurances are obtained from each consumer reporting agency that they are

complying with all laws related to providing consumer credit information. It is evident that the credit reporting agencies, including [Credit Bureau Name], have failed to obtain satisfactory assurances and comply with the relevant laws.

I want to reiterate that the violations of both the FCRA and the Privacy Act are serious matters. The credit reporting agencies have a legal obligation to protect consumer information and ensure compliance with federal laws governing the use and disclosure of that information.

Failure to comply with the provisions of the FCRA and the Privacy Act may result in severe legal consequences, including but not limited to:

1. FCRA Penalties for Willful Non-Compliance: Violations of the FCRA can result in statutory damages ranging from $100 to $1,000 per violation, depending on the severity of the violation. In cases of willful non-compliance, additional punitive damages may be awarded by the court.

2. Privacy Act Penalties and Fines: Violations of the Privacy Act of 1974 may result in penalties and fines, as specified under 5 U.S. Code § 552a(g). Individuals harmed by the violations may seek legal remedies and recover damages, including actual damages, attorney's fees, and court costs.

violations of 5 U.S. Code § 552a(g) of the Privacy Act of 1974:

1. Actual Damages: Individuals harmed by Privacy Act violations may seek to recover actual damages caused by the non-compliance. Actual damages refer to the specific financial losses or harm suffered as a result of the violation.

2. Statutory Damages: In addition to actual damages, individuals may be entitled to seek statutory damages as specified under 5 U.S. Code § 552a(g)(4)(A). The court may award statutory damages of up to $1,000 per violation.

3. Attorney's Fees and Court Costs: If successful in a legal action against the credit reporting agencies, individuals may be entitled to recover their reasonable attorney's fees and court costs incurred in pursuing the case.

It is crucial that the credit reporting agencies address these violations promptly and take necessary steps to rectify the situation. I demand a thorough investigation into these matters, a comprehensive response addressing the violations outlined, and written confirmation of the actions taken to rectify the inaccuracies on my credit report and ensure future compliance with all applicable laws.

Your immediate attention to this matter is essential. I anticipate a prompt and satisfactory resolution.

[Your Name]

[Your Contact Information: Phone Number and Email Address]

Enclosures:
- Copy of Credit Report
Supporting Documentation

NOTE: MAILING ADDRESS
Here are the dispute mailing addresses for Equifax, TransUnion, and Experian:

Equifax Information Services LLC
P.O. Box 740256
Atlanta, GA 30374-0256

TransUnion LLC
Consumer Dispute Center
P.O. Box 2000
Chester, PA 19016

Experian
P.O. Box 4500
Allen, TX 75013

When sending your dispute documents, it is recommended to use certified mail with a return receipt requested. This will provide proof of delivery and ensure that someone at the credit bureau signs for and receives the documents.

Mailing addresses and the names of the CEOs for Equifax, TransUnion, and Experian in the USA:

Equifax Inc.
Attn: Mark W. Begor (CEO)
1550 Peachtree Street NW
Atlanta, GA 30309

TransUnion LLC
Attn: Christopher A. Cartwright (CEO)
555 West Adams Street
Chicago, IL 60661

Experian Information Solutions Inc.
Attn: Craig Boundy (CEO)
475 Anton Boulevard
Costa Mesa, CA 92626

Please note that while these addresses are for their respective headquarters, it's important to consult with legal professionals or follow proper legal procedures for any legal actions or notices of intent to sue.

STEP 3 CREDIT DISPUTE LETTER

Note: (Include ID, Utility bill or proof of address and proof of social security number example Tax Document, SS Card)

Certified Mail #. 3638 8383 0303 3030 (signed PS 3800 or Electronic Signature check on PS 3800)
[Your Name]
[Your Address]
[City, State, ZIP Code]
[Date]

[Credit Bureau Name]
[Credit Bureau Address]
[City, State, ZIP Code]

Credit Report #

Notice Of Default and Intent to Sue

Dear [Credit Bureau Name],

I am writing this Notice of Default and Intent to Sue as a result of your continued failure to comply with the Fair Credit Reporting Act (FCRA), Privacy Act of 1974, and applicable copyright laws. Despite my previous correspondence and attempts to resolve the matter amicably, you have not completed the proper investigation, nor have you addressed the violations and concerns raised. This default notice serves as a final opportunity for you to rectify the situation before legal action is pursued.

The violations committed by [Credit Bureau Name] are as follows:

1. Violations of the Fair Credit Reporting Act (FCRA):

- Failure to conduct a reasonable investigation into disputed items (Section 611)
- Failure to remove inaccurate or unverifiable information (Section 611)
- Failure to provide written notification of investigation results (Section 611)
- Failure to correct inaccurate information (Section 611)
- Failure to comply with consumer reporting requirements (Section 623)
- Failure to properly handle disputes (Section 623)
- Failure to provide notice of dispute to information furnishers (Section 623)
- Failure to investigate and report disputed information (Section 623)
- Failure to notify consumers of negative information (Section 623)
- Failure to maintain reasonable procedures to ensure accuracy (Section 623)

2. Violations of the Privacy Act of 1974 (5 U.S. Code § 552a):

- Unauthorized disclosure of personal records without written consent (Section 552a(b))
- Failure to obtain prior written consent for disclosure to consumer reporting agencies (Section 552a(b)(12))
- Failure to comply with Section 3711(e) of Title 31, including failure to obtain satisfactory assurances from consumer reporting agencies regarding compliance with relevant laws

3. Violations of Copyright Laws:

- Unauthorized use of my private, copyrighted information without consent or just compensation

The consequences of your willful non-compliance with the aforementioned laws are severe and include but are not limited to the following:

1. Statutory damages for FCRA violations: Up to $1,000 per violation (Section 616)

2. Actual damages for FCRA violations: Any actual financial losses suffered as a result of the violations
3. Punitive damages for willful violations of the FCRA

4. Statutory damages for Privacy Act violations: Up to $1,000 per violation (Section 552a(g)(4)(A))

5. Actual damages for Privacy Act violations: Any actual financial losses or harm suffered as a result of the violations

6. Attorney's fees and court costs associated with legal action

7. Damages associated with unauthorized use of copyrighted information

Attached to this notice, you will find an Arbitration Application, Fee Schedule for Violations of Trust Property, and a copy of the previously sent correspondence. It is imperative that you review and consider these documents seriously.

You are hereby given a final opportunity to settle this matter outside of court by contacting me within 10 days from the date of this notice. Failure to respond or properly address the violations and concerns raised will be interpreted as a refusal to resolve the matter amicably. In such case, I will proceed with filing a lawsuit seeking judgment for the violations, damages, and all associated costs.

Please be advised that any failure to respond, properly answer discovery requests, or engage in good faith resolution discussions will be noted and presented to the court as evidence of your non-compliance and disregard for the legal process.

This Notice of Default and Intent to Sue is not to be taken lightly. I urge you to consider the severity of the violations and the potential consequences of continued non-compliance.

Sincerely,

[Your Name]

[Your Contact Information: Phone Number and Email Address]

Enclosures:

- Copy of Previous Correspondence
- Arbitration Application

Fee Schedule for Violations of Trust Property

NOTE: MAILING ADDRESS

Here are the dispute mailing addresses for Equifax, TransUnion, and Experian:

Equifax Information Services LLC
P.O. Box 740256
Atlanta, GA 30374-0256

TransUnion LLC
Consumer Dispute Center
P.O. Box 2000
Chester, PA 19016

Experian
P.O. Box 4500
Allen, TX 75013

When sending your dispute documents, it is recommended to use certified mail with a return receipt requested. This will provide proof of delivery and ensure that someone at the credit bureau signs for and receives the documents.

Mailing addresses and the names of the CEOs for Equifax, TransUnion, and Experian in the USA:

Equifax Inc.
Attn: Mark W. Begor (CEO)
1550 Peachtree Street NW
Atlanta, GA 30309

TransUnion LLC
Attn: Christopher A. Cartwright (CEO)
555 West Adams Street
Chicago, IL 60661

Experian Information Solutions Inc.
Attn: Craig Boundy (CEO)
475 Anton Boulevard
Costa Mesa, CA 92626

Please note that while these addresses are for their respective headquarters, it's important to consult with legal professionals or follow proper legal procedures for any legal actions or notices of intent to sue.

STEP 4 AFFIDAVIT

Note: (Include ID, Utility bill or proof of address and proof of social security number example Tax Document, SS Card)

Certified Mail #. 3638 8383 0303 3030 (signed PS 3800 or Electronic Signature check on PS 3800)
[Your Name]
[Your Address]
[City, State, ZIP Code]
[Date]

[Credit Bureau Name]
[Credit Bureau Address]
[City, State, ZIP Code]

Credit Report #

Affidavit Of Administrative Summary Judgment

[Your Name]
[Your Address]
[City, State, ZIP Code]
[Date]

Affidavit of Administrative Summary Judgment

State of [State]
County of [County]

Before me, a Notary Public in and for the State and County aforesaid, personally appeared [Your Name], known to me to be the affiant whose name is subscribed to the foregoing instrument, and being duly sworn, deposes and says:

1. I am the affiant in this matter and have personal knowledge of the facts stated herein.

2. On [Date], I sent a certified mail correspondence to [Credit Bureau Name] addressing the inaccuracies and violations of the Fair Credit Reporting Act (FCRA), Privacy Act of 1974, and applicable copyright laws.

3. A second certified mail correspondence was sent on [Date] to follow up on the previous dispute and raise additional concerns regarding their non-compliance and failure to address the violations and issues raised.

4. On [Date], a third certified mail correspondence was sent to [Credit Bureau Name] as a Notice of Default and Intent to Sue, emphasizing their continued non-compliance and refusal to resolve the matter amicably.

5. Despite the aforementioned correspondences sent via certified mail, [Credit Bureau Name] failed to adequately address the violations and concerns raised, and they did not provide a proper response or conduct a reasonable investigation as required by law.

6. Based on the willful non-compliance of [Credit Bureau Name] and their failure to properly address the violations, I assert that they agree to adhere to the violations listed in the previous correspondences and acknowledge their responsibility to pay the fees, damages, costs, and any other expenses deemed just and proper by the court.

7. It is further requested that [Credit Bureau Name] agrees to restore my good name, provide injunctive relief, and take all necessary actions to rectify the inaccuracies on my credit report resulting from their non-compliance and violations of the FCRA and Privacy Act.

8. I affirm that the facts stated in this Affidavit of Administrative Summary Judgment are true and correct to the best of my knowledge and belief.

IN WITNESS WHEREOF, I have hereunto set my hand and affixed my official seal on this [Date] day of [Month], [Year].

[Your Name]
Affiant

[Notary Public]
Notary Public, State of [State]
My Commission Expires: [Expiration Date]

[Notary Seal]

NOTE: MAILING ADDRESS
Here are the dispute mailing addresses for Equifax, TransUnion, and Experian:

Equifax Information Services LLC
P.O. Box 740256
Atlanta, GA 30374-0256

TransUnion LLC
Consumer Dispute Center
P.O. Box 2000
Chester, PA 19016
Experian
P.O. Box 4500
Allen, TX 75013

When sending your dispute documents, it is recommended to use certified mail with a return receipt requested. This will provide proof of delivery and ensure that someone at the credit bureau signs for and receives the documents.

Mailing addresses and the names of the CEOs for Equifax, TransUnion, and Experian in the USA:

Equifax Inc.
Attn: Mark W. Begor (CEO)
1550 Peachtree Street NW
Atlanta, GA 30309

TransUnion LLC
Attn: Christopher A. Cartwright (CEO)
555 West Adams Street
Chicago, IL 60661

Experian Information Solutions Inc.
Attn: Craig Boundy (CEO)
475 Anton Boulevard
Costa Mesa, CA 92626

Please note that while these addresses are for their respective headquarters, it's important to consult with legal professionals or follow proper legal procedures for any legal actions or notices of intent to sue.

STEP 5 CFPB CLAIM

Certified Mail #. 3638 8383 0303 3030 (signed PS 3800 or Electronic Signature check on PS 3800)
[Your Name]
[Your Address]
[City, State, ZIP Code]
[Date]

[Consumer Financial Protection Bureau]
[CFPB Address]
[City, State, ZIP Code]

RE: Equifax, Transunion, Experian Credit Report #

Formal Complaint and Notice of Violations- Request for Investigation

[Your Name]
[Your Address]
[City, State, ZIP Code]
[Date]

Consumer Financial Protection Bureau
[CFPB Address]
[City, State, ZIP Code]

Subject: Formal Complaint and Notice of Violations - Request for Investigation

Dear Consumer Financial Protection Bureau,

I am writing to file a formal complaint and bring to your attention the numerous violations committed by [Credit Bureau Name] regarding the Fair Credit Reporting Act (FCRA), Privacy Act of 1974, and other applicable laws. I believe their actions warrant an investigation and appropriate action to rectify the violations and protect consumers from further harm.

Summary of CLAIM:

1. Violations of the Fair Credit Reporting Act (FCRA):

- Failure to conduct a reasonable investigation into disputed items (Section 611) - Statutory damages of up to $1,000 per violation.
- Failure to remove inaccurate or unverifiable information (Section 611) - Actual damages and potential punitive damages.
- Failure to provide written notification of investigation results (Section 611) - Statutory damages of up to $1,000 per violation.
- Failure to correct inaccurate information (Section 611) - Actual damages and potential punitive damages.
- Failure to comply with consumer reporting requirements (Section 623) - Statutory damages of up to $1,000 per violation.
- Failure to properly handle disputes (Section 623) - Statutory damages of up to $1,000 per violation.
- Failure to provide notice of dispute to information furnishers (Section 623) - Statutory damages of up to $1,000 per violation.
- Failure to investigate and report disputed information (Section 623) - Statutory damages of up to $1,000 per violation.
- Failure to notify consumers of negative information (Section 623) - Statutory damages of up to $1,000 per violation.
- Failure to maintain reasonable procedures to ensure accuracy (Section 623) - Statutory damages of up to $1,000 per violation.

2. Violations of the Privacy Act of 1974 (5 U.S. Code § 552a):

- Unauthorized disclosure of personal records without written consent (Section 552a(b)) - Actual damages and potential punitive damages.
- Failure to obtain prior written consent for disclosure to consumer reporting agencies (Section 552a(b)(12)) - Actual damages and potential punitive damages.
- Failure to comply with Section 3711(e) of Title 31 - Applicable fines and penalties as determined by the court.

3. Violations of Copyright Laws:

- Unauthorized use of private, copyrighted information without consent or just compensation - Actual damages and potential punitive damages as determined by the court.

Timeline of Events and Correspondence:

1. [Date]: Initial dispute letter sent via certified mail to [Credit Bureau Name], outlining the inaccuracies and violations on my credit report.

- Certified Mail Receipt: [Receipt Number]

2. [Date]: Follow-up dispute letter sent via certified mail, addressing the continued non-compliance and failure to properly address the violations and concerns raised.

- Certified Mail Receipt: [Receipt Number]

3. [Date]: Notice of Default and Intent to Sue sent via certified mail, highlighting the willful non-compliance and refusal to resolve the matter amicably.
- Certified Mail Receipt: [Receipt Number]

Despite the certified mail correspondences and clear evidence of the violations, [Credit Bureau Name] has failed to adequately address the concerns, conduct a proper investigation, or provide a satisfactory resolution.

Requested Actions and Relief Sought:

1. Conduct a thorough investigation into the actions of [Credit Bureau Name] regarding the violations outlined above, including their failure to comply with the FCRA, Privacy Act of 1974, and copyright laws.

2. Impose appropriate penalties and fines as permitted by law for their willful non-compliance and violations.

3. Ensure that [Credit Bureau Name] takes immediate action to rectify the inaccuracies on my credit report, restore my good name, and implement measures to prevent further violations.

4. Request the court to order [Credit Bureau Name] to pay all costs, fees, and expenses incurred as a result of their breach and non-compliance, including but not limited to:

- Attorney's fees and court costs associated with legal action
- Damages associated with unauthorized use of copyrighted information

- Statutory damages for FCRA violations - Up to $1,000 per violation
- Actual damages for FCRA violations - Determined by the court
- Statutory damages for Privacy Act violations - Determined by the court
- Actual damages for Privacy Act violations - Determined by the court
- Any additional costs deemed just and proper by the court

5. Provide me with updates on the progress of the investigation and any actions taken as a result.

I have attached copies of the certified mail receipts, previous correspondences, and supporting documentation for your reference. I appreciate your attention to this matter and trust that the Consumer Financial Protection Bureau will take appropriate action to protect consumers and ensure compliance with the relevant laws.

Thank you for your prompt attention to this complaint. I look forward to a satisfactory resolution of this matter.

Sincerely,

[Your Name]
[Your Contact Information: Phone Number and Email Address]

Enclosures:

- Copy of Certified Mail Receipts
- Copies of Previous Correspondences
- Supporting Documentation

NOTE: MAILING ADDRESS

Here are the dispute mailing addresses for Equifax, TransUnion, and Experian:

Equifax Information Services LLC
P.O. Box 740256
Atlanta, GA 30374-0256

TransUnion LLC
Consumer Dispute Center
P.O. Box 2000
Chester, PA 19016

Experian
P.O. Box 4500
Allen, TX 75013

When sending your dispute documents, it is recommended to use certified mail with a return receipt requested. This will provide proof of delivery and ensure that someone at the credit bureau signs for and receives the documents.

Mailing addresses and the names of the CEOs for Equifax, TransUnion, and Experian in the USA:

Equifax Inc.
Attn: Mark W. Begor (CEO)
1550 Peachtree Street NW
Atlanta, GA 30309

TransUnion LLC
Attn: Christopher A. Cartwright (CEO)
555 West Adams Street
Chicago, IL 60661

Experian Information Solutions Inc.

Attn: Craig Boundy (CEO)
475 Anton Boulevard
Costa Mesa, CA 92626

CFPB
Consumer Financial Protection Bureau
1700 G Street NW
Washington, D.C. 20552

or file online The website to file a complaint with the Consumer Financial Protection Bureau (CFPB) is:

https://www.consumerfinance.gov/complaint/

Please note that while these addresses are for their respective headquarters, it's important to consult with legal professionals or follow proper legal procedures for any legal actions or notices of intent to sue.

STEP 6 NOTICE OF CLAIM

Certified Mail #. 3638 8383 0303 3030 (signed PS 3800 or Electronic Signature check on

[Your Name]
[Your Address]
[City, State, ZIP Code]
[Date]

Clerk of Court
United States District Court
Northern District of Georgia
[Court Address]
[City, State, ZIP Code]

Re: Civil Action No. [Case Number]
Plaintiff: [Your Name]
Defendant: [Credit Bureau Name]

Claim for Violations of Federal Laws, Georgia Constitution, and United States Constitution, and Relief Sought

Dear Clerk of Court,

I, [Your Name], the plaintiff in the above-captioned matter, hereby submit this claim pursuant to the Federal Rules of Civil Procedure, invoking the jurisdiction of this honorable court. This claim seeks redress for the numerous violations committed by [Credit Bureau Name] against the plaintiff, including violations of federal laws, the Georgia Constitution, the United States Constitution, and the resulting injuries.

I. Jurisdiction and Venue

This claim falls within the jurisdiction of this honorable court under the applicable provisions of the United States Constitution and federal laws, including but not limited to 28 U.S.C. § 1331 (federal question jurisdiction). The Northern District of Georgia is the appropriate venue for this claim as it relates to the actions and operations of [Credit Bureau Name] within this district.

II. Statement of Claim

Count 1: Violations of Federal Laws

a. [Credit Bureau Name] willfully failed to comply with the provisions of the Fair Credit Reporting Act (FCRA) as outlined in 15 U.S.C. § 1681 et seq., including but not limited to Sections 611 and 623.

b. [Credit Bureau Name] knowingly neglected to comply with the requirements of the Privacy Act of 1974 (5 U.S. Code § 552a).

c. [Credit Bureau Name] intentionally violated the plaintiff's rights under the Fourth Amendment of the United States Constitution, as it pertains to the unauthorized use and disclosure of private property without consent or just compensation.

Count 2: Violations of Georgia Constitution

a. [Credit Bureau Name] violated the plaintiff's rights under the Georgia Constitution, including but not limited to Article I, Section I (Protection to person and property), Article I, Section II (Right to trial by jury), and Article I, Section III (Protection against unreasonable searches and seizures).

III. Relief Sought

Based on the aforementioned violations and resulting injuries, the plaintiff seeks the following relief:

1. Compensatory Damages:

a. Actual damages for the harm suffered as a direct result of the violations committed by [Credit Bureau Name].

2. Statutory Damages:

a. Statutory damages as provided by applicable federal laws.

3. Punitive Damages:

a. Punitive damages for the willful non-compliance and disregard for the plaintiff's rights and constitutional protections.

4. Injunctive Relief:

a. Immediate removal of inaccuracies from the plaintiff's credit report.

b. Implementation of robust procedures to ensure compliance with federal laws and regulations

5. Declaratory Judgment:

a. A declaration that [Credit Bureau Name]'s actions and conduct are repugnant to the United States Constitution and the Georgia Constitution.

6. Attorney's Fees and Costs:

a. Recovery of all reasonable attorney's fees and costs associated with pursuing this claim.

IV. Federal Questions Presented

1. Whether [Credit Bureau Name]'s actions and conduct, in violation of federal laws, the Georgia Constitution, and the United States Constitution, warrant redress under federal jurisdiction.

2. Whether the plaintiff is entitled to compensatory damages, statutory damages, punitive damages, injunctive relief, declaratory judgment, and attorney's fees and costs based on the aforementioned violations and resulting injuries.

V. Exhibits

The following exhibits are attached herewith and incorporated by reference into this complaint:

a. Exhibit A: Notice of Default and Intent to Sue

b. Exhibit B: Affidavit of Administrative Summary Judgment

c. Exhibit C: Correspondence Sent to [Credit Bureau Name]

d. Exhibit D: Certified Mail Receipts

e. Exhibit E: Other Relevant Supporting Documents

VI. Conclusion

Accordingly, I respectfully request that this claim be filed and processed in accordance with the Federal Rules of Civil Procedure and applicable laws. I further request that a copy of this claim, along with the attached exhibits, be served upon the defendant, [Credit Bureau Name], in accordance with the established procedures of this court.

Thank you for your attention to this matter.

Sincerely,

[Your Name]

NOTE: PARTIES TO BE SERVED AND MAILING ADDRESS FIND THERE LEGAL REPRESENTATIVE

Mailing addresses and the names of the CEOs for Equifax, TransUnion, and Experian in the USA:

Equifax Inc.
Attn: Mark W. Begor (CEO)
1550 Peachtree Street NW
Atlanta, GA 30309

TransUnion LLC
Attn: Christopher A. Cartwright (CEO)
555 West Adams Street
Chicago, IL 60661

Experian Information Solutions Inc.
Attn: Craig Boundy (CEO)

475 Anton Boulevard
Costa Mesa, CA 92626

Please note that while these addresses are for their respective headquarters, it's important to consult with legal professionals or follow proper legal procedures for any legal actions or notices of intent to sue.

STEP 7 THE CLAIM

IN THE UNITED STATES DISTRICT COURT
FOR THE NORTHERN DISTRICT OF GEORGIA

[Your Name],
Plaintiff,

v.

[Credit Bureau Name],
Defendant.

Case No.: [Case Number]

CLAIM

Plaintiff, [Your Name], brings this action against [Credit Bureau Name] (hereinafter referred to as "Defendant"), and states as follows:

I. JURISDICTION AND VENUE

1. This Court has subject matter jurisdiction over this action pursuant to 28 U.S.C. § 1331, as the claims alleged herein arise under federal laws, including the Fair Credit Reporting Act (FCRA), the Privacy Act of 1974, and copyright laws.

2. Venue is proper in this district pursuant to 28 U.S.C. § 1391(b), as a substantial part of the events or omissions giving rise to the claims occurred within this district and Defendant conducts business within this district.

II. PARTIES

3. Plaintiff, [Your Name], is an individual residing at [Your Address], [City, State, ZIP Code].

4. Defendant, [Credit Bureau Name], is a credit reporting agency incorporated under the laws of [State of Incorporation] and conducting business within the Northern District of Georgia.

III. STATEMENT OF CLAIMS

Count 1: Violation of the Fair Credit Reporting Act (FCRA)

a. [Credit Bureau Name] willfully failed to comply with the provisions of the FCRA, specifically Sections 611 and 623, by neglecting to conduct a reasonable investigation into disputed items, failing to correct or remove inaccurate information, and mishandling disputes.

b. Plaintiff is entitled to relief under the FCRA, as these violations have caused harm and injury.

Count 2: Violation of the Privacy Act of 1974 (5 U.S. Code § 552a)

a. [Credit Bureau Name] knowingly and unlawfully disclosed Plaintiff's personal records without written consent, in violation of Section 552a(b) of the Privacy Act.

b. Plaintiff is entitled to relief under the Privacy Act, as the unauthorized disclosure of personal records has resulted in damages and invasion of privacy.

Count 3: Violation of Copyright Laws

a. [Credit Bureau Name] used Plaintiff's copyrighted information without consent or just compensation, in violation of federal copyright laws.

b. Plaintiff is entitled to relief under copyright laws, as Defendant's unauthorized use of copyrighted information has caused financial loss and infringement of intellectual property rights.

IV. FEDERAL QUESTION

Does the conduct of [Credit Bureau Name], as alleged in Counts 1, 2, and 3, violate the Constitution of the United States, specifically the First, Fourth, Fifth, and Fourteenth Amendments? If so, are the violations in line with the Constitution, or are they repugnant to the Constitution?

V. RELIEF SOUGHT

1. Compensatory Damages:

a. Actual damages for the harm suffered as a direct result of the violations committed by [Credit Bureau Name].

b. Damages associated with the unauthorized use of copyrighted information.

2. Statutory Damages:

a. Statutory damages as provided by the FCRA, the Privacy Act of 1974, and copyright laws.

3. Punitive Damages:

a. Punitive damages to deter [Credit Bureau Name] from engaging in similar misconduct in the future.

4. Injunctive Relief:

a. Immediate removal of inaccuracies from Plaintiff's credit report.

b. Implementation of comprehensive procedures to ensure compliance with federal laws and regulations.

c. Prohibition of the unauthorized use of copyrighted information.

5. Declaratory Judgment:

a. A declaration that [Credit Bureau Name]'s actions and conduct are in violation of federal laws and constitutional rights.

6. Attorney's Fees and Costs:

a. Recovery of all reasonable attorney's fees and costs incurred as a result of pursuing this claim.

VI. DEMAND FOR JURY BY JURY

Plaintiff demands a trial by jury on all claims so triable.

VII. EXHIBITS

The following exhibits are attached herewith and incorporated by reference into this Complaint:

a. Exhibit A: Notice of Default and Intent to Sue

b. Exhibit B: Affidavit of Administrative Summary Judgment

c. Exhibit C: Correspondence Sent to [Credit Bureau Name]

d. Exhibit D: Certified Mail Receipts

e. Exhibit E: Other Relevant Supporting Documents

VIII. DEMAND FOR RELIEF

WHEREFORE, Plaintiff requests that this Court enter judgment against Defendant and grant the following relief:

1. Compensatory damages, statutory damages, and punitive damages as determined by the Court.

2. Injunctive relief to remedy the violations and prevent future harm.

3. Declaratory judgment declaring Defendant's actions to be in violation of federal laws and constitutional rights.

4. Attorney's fees and costs.

5. Such other and further relief as the Court deems just and proper.

Respectfully submitted,

[Your Name]
[Your Address]
[City, State, ZIP Code]
[Phone Number]
[Email Address]

DATED: [Date]

CERTIFICATE OF SERVICE

I, [Your Name], hereby certify that on [Date], I served the following documents upon [Credit Bureau Name] by certified mail, with a return receipt requested: Certified mail number: 44646464646464646464

1. Complaint

2. Exhibits:

a. Exhibit A: Notice of Default and Intent to Sue

b. Exhibit B: Affidavit of Administrative Summary Judgment

c. Exhibit C: Correspondence Sent to [Credit Bureau Name]

d. Exhibit D: Certified Mail Receipts

e. Exhibit E: Other Relevant Supporting Documents

The documents were sent to the following address:

[Equifax Inc.]
Attn: Mark W. Begor (CEO)
1550 Peachtree Street NW
Atlanta, GA 30309

Registered Agent Corporation Service Company 2 Sun Court, suite 400, Peachtree Corners, GA, 30092, USA]

I affirm that the above-mentioned documents were enclosed in a sealed envelope and deposited with the

United States Postal Service, with postage fully prepaid, and addressed as stated above.

I further confirm that the certified mail receipts, bearing the corresponding tracking numbers, are attached herewith as proof of service.

DATED: [Date]

____

[Your Name]

NOTE: PARTIES TO BE SERVED AND MAILING ADDRESS FIND THERE Registered Agents.

Mailing addresses and the names of the CEOs for Equifax, TransUnion, and Experian in the USA:

Equifax Inc.
Attn: Mark W. Begor (CEO)
1550 Peachtree Street NW
Atlanta, GA 30309

Registered Agent Corporation Service Company 2 Sun Court, suite 400, Peachtree Corners, GA, 30092, USA

TransUnion LLC
Attn: Christopher A. Cartwright (CEO)
555 West Adams Street
Chicago, IL 60661

Registered Agent Corporation Service Company 2 Sun Court, suite 400, Peachtree Corners, GA, 30092, USA

Experian Information Solutions Inc.
Attn: Craig Boundy (CEO)
475 Anton Boulevard
Costa Mesa, CA 92626

Registered Agent CT Corporation System 289 S Culver St, Lawrenceville, GA 30046-4805, USA

Please note that while these addresses are for their respective headquarters, it's important to consult with legal professionals or follow proper legal procedures for any legal actions or notices of intent to sue.

WELCOME TO THE CREDIT POWER HOUSE

Congratulations! You are now prepared to embark on the Credit Power House journey. If you haven't read all the sections in this book, I highly recommend going back to ensure you grasp the principles that underlie the upcoming steps. The upcoming training workshop offers numerous benefits as it will provide a comprehensive understanding of why our approach works while others may fall short. This workshop will guide you through a 10-step process that guarantees results and financial gains. Don't miss out—click the link below and join me on the other side. Get ready to transform your credit journey! Looking forward to seeing you there!

Editors Note:

As we come to the end of "Credit Power House," we would like to express our gratitude to our dedicated team of writers, researchers, and editors who have worked tirelessly to bring you this comprehensive guide to understanding credit and mastering your financial journey. Throughout this series, we have explored various aspects of credit, from building a solid credit history to managing debts and improving credit scores. Our goal has been to empower our readers with the knowledge and tools necessary to make informed financial decisions and achieve their credit goals. We hope that "Credit Power House" has provided you with valuable insights, practical tips, and a deeper understanding of the complex world of credit. Remember, credit plays a vital role in many aspects of our lives, from purchasing a home or car to accessing affordable loans and credit cards. By taking control of your credit and making wise choices, you can pave the way for a more secure financial future. We understand that everyone's credit journey is unique, and while this series covers a wide range of topics, there may be specific situations or questions that require personalized advice. We encourage you to consult with qualified professionals, such as financial advisors or credit counselors, who can provide tailored guidance based on your individual circumstances. At Credit Power House, our commitment is to continue providing you with reliable and up-to-date information to support your ongoing financial education. We welcome your feedback, suggestions, and ideas for future topics you would like us to explore. Thank you for joining us on this credit exploration. Remember, knowledge is power, and with the right tools and understanding, you have the ability to unlock the full potential of your credit and achieve your financial goals. Best regards, The Credit Power House Editorial Team.

®is a registered trademark of Yunis Adon El Express Trust. All rights reserved. This logo is a registered trademark in the United States and may not be used or reproduced without prior written permission from the trademark owner. For inquiries regarding the use of this trademark,
please contact: support@thecreditpowerhouse.com

Made in United States
Cleveland, OH
05 November 2026

47644436R00063